Christmas Memories

Christmas Memories © 2024 Alissa Goudy

ISBN# 978-1-998532-11-7

1. Christmas. Holiday 3. Seasonal

Published by Ahelia Publishing, LLC

Printed in the USA

Christmas Memories

by Alissa Goudy

Christmas memories
made far or near,
The perfect season
for love and cheer.

Lasting memories
shimmer in our eyes,
As you gaze upon
the dancing skies.

Memories of an enchanted winter wonderland,
With snowflakes dancing and wonder grande.

Frost glistens under
the silver moonlight,
Snow-covered branches
and lights twinkle bright.

Hayrides and carolers
singing with glee,
With rosy-red cheeks
from the cold winter breeze.

In the old barn

shaped like an Inn,

Before your eyes

the festivities begin.

While flickering candles
give off a cheerful glow,
A simple wreath hangs
with a neatly tied bow.

Green festive garland drapes
upon each window neatly,
As the scent of cranberry and
cinnamon fills the air sweetly.

Candy canes and gumdrops fill little cheeks. The children are delighted after waiting for weeks.

As they whisper and giggle
making houses of gingerbread,
They will forever remember
these Christmases on
the old homestead.

Roast marshmallows or chestnuts at your heart's desire,
As you gather around a warm, open fire.

Hot cocoa with peppermint to keep our hands warm,
Before your eyes, hearts will transform.

With comfort and joy your
heart will soon feel it,
This is the true meaning
of the Christmas Spirit.

As you gather around
this Christmas Eve,
Have a child-like heart
and fully believe.

Let us embrace

this joyous opportunity,

To create the perfect

place for peace and unity.

Some hope and peace
I leave with you now,
As a light inside you
will ignite with a glow.

Your greatest blessings will always be, Surrounding yourself with friends and family.

From my home to yours,

Merry Christmas.

Printed in the USA
CPSIA information can be obtained
at www.ICGtesting.com
LVHW071732051024
792941LV00004B/11